BREAKING HABITS

Learning To Live In Freedom!

BREAKING HABITS

Learning To Live In Freedom!

BOB GASS
with Ruth Gass Halliday

DEDICATION

This book is dedicated to Bill Reilly who has worked with thousands of hurting people, helping them to find freedom from destructive habits and discover a quality of life they never dreamed possible.

I know, I was one of them.

Breaking Habits

All Scripture used in this book are King James Version unless otherwise indicated.

Scripture quotations marked AMP are taken from *The Amplified Bible, Old Testament*. Copyright © 1965, 1987 by the Zondervan Corporation. *The Amplified New Testament*, copyright © 1954, 1958, 1987 by the Lockman Foundation. Used by permission.

Scripture quotations marked CEV are taken from the *Contemporary English Version*, copyright © 1995, 1999 by American Bible Society, New York. Used by permission.

Scripture quotations marked NAS are from the *New American Standard Bible*. Copyright © 1960, 1962, 1963, 1968, 1971, 1972, 1975, 1977 by the Lockman Foundation. Used by permission.

Scripture quotations marked NCV are taken from *The Holy Bible, New Century Version*, copyright © 1987, 1988, 1991 by Word Publishing, Dallas, Texas 75234. Used by permission.

Scripture quotations marked NIV are taken from the *Holy Bible: New International Version*. Copyright © 1973, 1978, 1984 by the International Bible Society. Used by permission of Zondervan Bible Publishers.

Scripture quotations marked NLT are taken from the *Holy Bible, New Living Translation*, copyright © 1996. Used by permission of Tyndale House Publishers, Inc., Wheaton, Illinois 60189. All rights reserved.

Scripture quotations marked NKJV are taken from the *New King James Version*. Copyright ©1979, 1980, 1982, Thomas Nelson Inc., Publishers. Used by permission.

Scripture quotations marked TLB are from *The Living Bible*. Copyright © 1971 by Tyndale House Publishers, Wheaton, IL. Used by permission.

Scripture quotations marked TM are from *The Message: The New Testament, Psalms and Proverbs*. Copyright © 1993, 1994, 1995, 1996 by Eugene H. Peterson. Used by permission of NavPress Publishing Group.

BREAKING HABITS: Learning To Live In Freedom
Copyright ©2002 by Celebration Enterprises
P.O. Box 1045
Roswell, GA 30077-1045
ISBN 1-931727-98-8

Synergy Publishers
Gainesville, Florida 32635

Printed in the United States of America. All rights reserved. Under International Copyright Law, no part of this publication may be reproduced, stored, or transmitted by any means—electronic, mechanical, photographic (photocopy), recording, or otherwise—without written permission from the Publisher.

Notice to our American and Canadian readers: This book has been "Anglicized" for the British market, therefore certain words are spelled differently.

Table of Contents

Introduction
Do You Have A Habit You Can't Break? 11
Be Honest 17
Be Realistic 19
Be Committed 21
Be Accountable 24
Don't Set Yourself Up 26
Don't Just Remove The Habit – Replace It 28
Cut The Cord! 31
Work On Your Self-Esteem 32
Help! I Miss My Old Habit 34
Walking On Water 36
Under Construction 38
Endurance – The Price Tag For Success 41
When You're Tempted To Go Back 43
It's A Daily Battle 46
Eight "Habit Breakers" 50

Introduction

Breaking habits begins with a "quality decision." To make that decision, you must want freedom more than you want your habit.

If that's where you are today, this book will help you!

1
Do You Have A Habit You Can't Break?

A habit is a problem, when just the *thought* or *suggestion*, causes us to give in to it.

The Bible refers to these habits as "strongholds," (things which have a strong hold on us) and tells us we have "power to demolish strongholds" (2 Cor 10:4 NIV).

Don't be fooled. Just because: (a) your habit hasn't been exposed; (b) you're not yet aware of any negative consequences resulting from it; (c) your conscience doesn't bother you about it; (d) lots of others do the same thing – doesn't mean you won't pay a high price for indulging in it.

Paul says, "Whatsoever a man soweth, that shall he also reap" (Gal 6:7). You won't necessarily reap where you sow or when you sow, but you'll always reap *what* you sow.

Breaking Habits

We all struggle with habits. What's yours? Be honest.

How's your *weight*? Sixty percent of us are now overweight, one in three are clinically obese (twenty percent over our ideal weight). The good times are killing us!

Do you have the *desire* and the *strength* (you must have both), to eliminate the wrong foods, start eating the right ones, reduce your portions, stop eating at bedtime, and begin exercising regularly?

Are you a smoker? If you are, the odds are stacked against you living out your days.

"But it's *my* life," you say.

What about those who love you and depend on you?

A woman wrote to columnist Ann Landers saying, "A few weeks ago our family gathered to bury one of the dearest most gentle people I have ever known. He was married for forty-three years to our eldest sister. He was a delight. We adored him. He was meticulous about detail, the perfect choice to take charge of any family project. Dependable. Industrious. Thorough. Integrity was his middle name. But this man who did everything right, did

Do You Have A Habit You Can't Break?

one thing wrong. He smoked at least two-packs a day for thirty years. This senseless addiction deprived him of the joy of seeing his grandchildren marry. It also denied those of us who loved him the pleasure of his beautiful presence. For God's sake and the sake of those who love you, stop smoking today. Do it for yourself. Do it for the people who care about you."

Do you drink too much? Does that question make you uncomfortable?

If you want to know whether you have a drinking problem, or a potential one, answer these questions.

(1) Do you need a drink at a definite time every day? (2) Do you prefer to drink alone? (3) In the morning do you crave "the hair of the dog that bit you?" (4) Is your drinking hurting your family in any way? (5) Do you take a drink when you feel yourself getting the shakes? (6) Is drinking damaging your reputation? (7) Do you lose time from work because of it? (8) Has it made you inconsiderate of your family's welfare? (9) Since drinking, have you become jealous or suspicious of your spouse? (10) Has your initiative and perseverance decreased? (11) Do you drink to

relieve anxiety? (12) Has your drinking made you more sensitive (touchy)? (13) Is it endangering your health? (14) Are you moody as a result of drinking? (15) Has it made you harder to get along with? (16) Is it making your home life unhappy? (17) Is it jeopardizing your job or hurting your business or career? (18) Has it made you irritable? (19) Is it affecting your peace of mind? (20) Has drinking caused you to have an accident? (21) Do you lie about your drinking and try to hide it from others?

If you can answer 'no' to every one of these questions, and a member of your family agrees, then your drinking is under control – at least for the present. Every 'yes' answer is a red light, meaning there could be trouble ahead.

How about pornography? Habits practiced in the dark have a way of breaking through into the light.

It happened some years ago to a prominent minister. His secret habit was exposed – twice! Afraid, alone, ashamed, he wrestled with it, preached against it, prayed over it, even rebuked it – but he failed!

When did his problem begin? As a teenager. Without realizing it, each time he picked up another magazine he filed a picture in his memory bank; a file the enemy would pull in moments of weakness and project on to the screen of his imagination, igniting desires and driving him to risk everything he held near and dear.

And for what? A few moments of mood-altering excitement and relief?

Even if you don't get blown out of the water, think what pornography does to your *mind*; the feelings of shame in its aftermath.

And what about the damage it does to your *marriage*? The fantasies? What marriage could live up to the "antics" performed by those on the screen? Nobody is unfaithful in their marriage, till they are first unfaithful in their mind.

Wise up, you're uncaging a force that has the potential to devour you.

How about gossip? "Are you serious?" Yes! The Bible has *more* to say about the destructive potential of an uncontrolled tongue, than all the habits we've mentioned so far.

Some habits can end your life; others can destroy your soul.

Breaking Habits

For most of us it's habits of *attitude* and *disposition* (cranky, critical, controlling etc.) that need to be dealt with, because those are the ones that keep us from growing, excelling, and soaring to the heights God planned for us.

Listen, "Let us throw off everything that *hinders* [stands in our way] and the sin that so easily *entangles* [trips us up], and let us run with perseverance the race marked out for us" (Heb 12:1 NIV).

The Psalmist wrote, "Search me, O God, and know my heart…See if there is any offensive *way* in me" (Ps 139:23-24 NIV). Habits are *"ways"* of thinking and acting that become part of our everyday lives; ways of trying to meet a need or fill a void.

The problem is, they're just symptoms of deeper, unresolved issues that need dealt with in healthier ways.

They're crutches; they're what we use to help us get through life.

When a habit becomes stronger than we are, we need help. And it's available because God is "a very present help in trouble" (Ps 46:1).

Do you have a habit you need to break? If so, read on.

2
BE HONEST

As long as you entertain the idea that *you* can break the habit in your own strength, nothing will change. If you could, you'd have done it by now, wouldn't you?

Furthermore, as long as you're operating in will power, you're disconnected from God's power!

It takes humility to acknowledge defeat, then surrender to God, but unless you do you'll get nowhere. Jesus said, "As the branch cannot bear fruit of itself, except it abide in the vine; no more can ye, except ye abide in me...for without me ye can do nothing" (Jn 15:4-5).

The trouble is, we read those words, go out and act like it all depends on us, fall flat on our face, and wonder why.

We must come to the place where we make a conscious decision *each day*, and sometimes *each hour*, to turn our life and our will over to God; to pray, "Lord, I don't have the ability to overcome this. I choose not to give in to it. Strengthen me now by Your Spirit."

That's a prayer God will answer. Why? Because He *always* empowers our choices when they line up with His will!

3
BE REALISTIC

We form our habits and then our habits form us. You didn't get into the shape you're in overnight, and you may not get out overnight either. But the longest road is shorter when you take your first step.

Some people testify that after prayer, counseling, or being ministered to by a particular person, their desires immediately change and their chains are broken.

Sometimes that happens, and it's wonderful!

Others, however, have to "walk it out," calling on God's grace *each day* (and sometimes each hour) in order to get through.

Paul wrote concerning his thorn in the flesh, "Three times I pleaded with the Lord to take it away from me. But he said to me, 'My grace is sufficient for you, for my power is made perfect in weakness.' Therefore I will boast all the more gladly about my weaknesses, so that Christ's power may rest on me…For when I am weak, then I am strong" (2 Cor 12:8-10 NIV).

The truth is, if it hadn't been for certain habits, many of us would never have *found* the Lord, or developed the *relationship* we enjoy with Him today. God uses our struggles to draw us closer to Him.

When we begin to see that, we will no longer waste time regretting the past or wishing to change it.

4
BE COMMITTED

Many of us use mood-altering things such as alcohol, drugs, food, sex, multiple-relationships and work, to "fix" ourselves. We carry so much pain beneath the surface – pain we haven't dealt with, because we don't know how.

We don't know how to feel our feelings, face reality, or live life on life's terms, so we seek escape. And we're only ready to give up our habit when it costs too much and rewards too little; when the pain becomes greater than the pleasure.

This is called *"hitting the bottom."*

Do you remember the story of *The Prodigal Son*? Listen, "The younger son…set off for a distant country, and there squandered his wealth in wild living…After he had spent everything, there was a severe famine…and he began to be in need."

Sound familiar? Read on:

"So he went and hired himself out to a citizen of that country, who sent him to his fields to feed pigs. He longed to fill his stomach with the pods that the pigs were eating, but no one gave him anything" (Lk 15:5-16 NIV).

Ever been there?

Most of us don't get off the elevator until it can go no lower. Read on:

"*When he came to his senses* [hit the bottom], he said…'I will…go back to my father and say to him: Father, I have sinned'" (Lk 15:17-18 NIV).

Your breaking point can be your turning point. Read on:

"But while he was still a long way off, his father saw him and was filled with compassion for him; he ran to his son, threw his arms around him and kissed him. The son said to him, 'Father, I have sinned against heaven and against you. I am no longer worthy to be called your son.' But the father said to his servants, 'Quick! Bring the best robe and put it on him. Put a ring on his finger and sandals on his feet. Bring the fattened calf and kill it. Let's have a feast and celebrate. For this son of mine was dead and is alive again; he was lost and is found.'" (Lk 15:20-24 NIV).

Usually we don't change until we get sick and tired of being sick and tired! Only then do we turn to God in earnest and commit ourselves to living *His* way.

Instead of singing, "He's all I need," we now realize, *"He's all I've got!"*

As long as you try to rationalise or defend your problem, you can't solve it. *Nothing* will change until you face it squarely, admit, "It's too big for me," and give it to God.

Don't worry about shocking Him, He already knows all about you. And the good news is, He doesn't just know what you *are*, He knows *what you can be* when His grace goes to work in your life.

5
BE ACCOUNTABLE

Solomon writes, "A friend loveth at all times, and a brother is born for adversity" (Prov 17:17).

Find someone *mature* enough to keep your confidence, *strong* enough to hold you accountable, and *committed* enough not to give up on you.

Listen, "Two people are better than one…If one falls down, the other can help him up. But it is bad for the person who is alone and falls, because no one is there to help" (Ecc 4:9-10 NCV).

Find a trustworthy friend who understands your problem, because they've successfully dealt with it themselves.

Make a commitment to call them *before* you get into trouble!

The difference between success and failure can be as little as five or ten minutes on the phone with someone who understands, because they've dealt with the same problem!

But look out!

Shame will whisper, "Don't you feel bad about always having to depend on somebody else?"

Deceit will whisper, "You failed too often. They'll get tired and give up on you. Wouldn't you, in their place?"

Fear will whisper, "Don't give anybody that kind of control over you."

Pride will whisper, "You don't need to tell them you blew it again. Just get up, dust yourself off and say nothing."

Don't listen to those voices. Reach for the help that's available!

6
DON'T SET YOURSELF UP

Learn to avoid the wrong people, places, and pleasures. It takes courage to say, "Others may, but I can't."

Recognise your "triggers."

Become aware of what's going on *around* you and *within* you each time you're tempted.

Every action begins as a thought. Before you surrender in reality, you first surrender in your *mind*. That's why Paul says, "Capture every thought… make it give up and obey Christ" (2 Cor 10:5 NCV).

If you struggle with alcohol don't eat in a bar. If you battle pornography don't linger around news stands or bring it into your home via TV or the Internet. If being with smokers' triggers you, explain to your friends that you can't be around them when they smoke. If they're true friends, they'll understand and support you.

Don't Set Yourself Up

If living habit-free is a serious commitment on your part – plan your life around that commitment!

The day may come when you'll be able to handle the pressure of old playmates and playgrounds, but in the early stages you need to avoid *anything* that threatens your commitment to living in freedom!

7
DON'T JUST REMOVE THE HABIT – REPLACE IT

If you don't you'll invariably go back to it.

How many times have you made a resolution to lose weight, stop smoking or drinking, curb your temper, _____ (*you fill in the blank*), only to find yourself failing again? Your *fresh starts* keep turning into *false starts*, and you end up discouraged and hopeless.

That's because you don't understand the difference between *redoing* and *renewing*!

To *redo* is to start over, using the same tools and the same approach. To renew is to begin again, using *new* tools and a *new* approach.

If you want what you don't have, you've got to do what you haven't done yet.

Here are two things you need to start practicing each day if you really want to change:

Don't Just Remove The Habit – Replace It

(a) *Give yourself fully to Christ.* Nothing will change until you do. Listen, "If anyone is in Christ, he is a new creation; the old has gone, the new has come" (2 Cor 5:17 NIV). God can do for you what you can't do for yourself, but you have to *ask* Him to do it! His power to help is released only when you request it!

(b) *Renew your mind.* Listen again, "Everything – connected with that old way of life has to go…Get rid of it…take on…a God-fashioned life, a life renewed from the inside…working itself [out] into your conduct as God…reproduces his character in you" (Eph 4:23-24 TM).

Start to replace your old thoughts with God's thoughts. David said, "I will study your commandments and reflect on your ways. I will delight in your principles and not forget your word" (Ps 119:15-16 NLT).

Did you get that? Study them! Reflect on them! Delight in them! Memorise them!

Bill Reilly heads up the *Overcomers Ministry* at the Cathedral of the Holy Spirit in Atlanta. During the last twenty years, he's worked with over fifteen thousand people recovering from various addictions. When asked the difference between those who succeed and those who fail, Bill said, "The successful ones do three things:

(1) They build themselves up spiritually by reading, praying, fellowshipping with others who are working a good programme of recovery, and attending church every time the doors are open.

(2) They get a sponsor – and use him.

(3) They get involved helping others. Instead of focusing on their own needs, they find a cause greater than themselves and pour their lives into it."

That's a formula that can't fail!

8
CUT THE CORD!

The *past* will always be the *present*, until you learn to deal with it God's way!

That way is the way of forgiveness; it involves forgiving others – and yourself!

Once you forgive, the debt is cancelled. Its power to influence you is broken.

That means you no longer need to "medicate" it!

This may mean going back and apologising to those you've hurt, seeking to make amends if possible, in order to "close the door."

Remember, the moment you forgive, you let *yourself* off the hook, you "depressurise" that area of irritation, restlessness, and compulsion, *removing the need to go back to your old habit!*

9
WORK ON YOUR SELF-ESTEEM

Each time you indulge in self-destructive behaviour you lose a little more self-respect.

What we value, we protect!

When you don't respect yourself you've no motivation to nurture yourself, or seek to maximize your God-given gifts.

As long as you run around thinking, "My life is just a mess," you'll expect only the worst.

Actually when God offers you new opportunities you'll reject them out of a sense of unworthiness. Or worse, you'll unconsciously sabotage them because of an old belief system that says, "Nothing good ever happens for me."

So long as you think and talk that way you'll remain *stuck* in your habit, because it gives you a *temporary* sense of relief or excitement.

What's the answer? Discover what *God* thinks

Work On Your Self-Esteem

about you!

Meditate on His Word daily! Confess it! This is called "renewing your mind" (See Rom 12:2). When you first begin to do it you'll feel like a walking contradiction. Your feelings, your memories, your old programming, will rise up and tell you you're being ridiculous.

Don't listen to them!

You are what *God* says you are! Your true value is the value *He* places on you!

10
HELP! I MISS MY OLD HABIT

Don't be surprised if you miss your old habit; especially if it's one you've had for a long time.

Smokers say when they quit, they don't know what to do with their fingers because they've always had a cigarette between them.

Problem drinkers are tempted with the thought of a cold beer on a hot summer day. Some say they can actually taste it!

Over-eaters discover that their biggest challenge is family members and friends who say, "Go ahead, eat! You can always go back on your diet tomorrow."

And the devil will whisper: (a) "It's not fair; others can enjoy it, why can't you?" (b) "Now that you've gone without it for a while, you've proven you're strong enough to enjoy it in moderation." (c) "Just because somebody else can't control it, doesn't mean you can't." (d) "If the Bible doesn't specifically say it's a sin, then it must be okay."

Your commitment to be free must be a *lifetime commitment*. And that commitment should be *reaffirmed in prayer at the beginning of each day*.

The moment you even *think* about using or indulging again, turn to God immediately, then call your sponsor or trusted friend.

James writes, "Submit yourselves therefore to God. Resist the devil, and he will flee from you" (Jas 4:7).

It's the *submitted* life that has the power to overcome!

11
WALKING ON WATER

Let's take another look at the miracle of Peter walking on the water, and see what we can learn.

Listen, "And when Peter was come down out of the ship, he walked on the water...But when he saw the wind...he was afraid; and beginning to sink, he cried, saying 'Lord, save me.' And...Jesus stretched forth his hand, and caught him" (Mt 14:29-31). Notice three things:

(1) *It takes more than one step to get there.* This wasn't a little two-person rowing boat where you just hop over the side. It was a large ship. To get to Jesus you had to climb over the side, keep walking, and keep your eyes on Him. In other words – persevere!

(2) *Nobody walks without fluctuation.* Notice the words "he walked," and "he was afraid." We all go through it! One moment it feels like we're walking,

the next like we're sinking. It's a learning process. Exercising your faith means learning to stand on the stuff you used to sink in; declaring, "I'm going from *talking* about the power of God – to *walking* in it."

(3) *God's power is for people who are going down.* Listen, "Jesus stretched forth his hand and caught him." If you fall, the Lord will be there to catch you! Anybody will invest in a company whose stock is going up, but God will invest in one that's going down! Listen, "He giveth power to the faint; and to them that have no might he increaseth strength" (Isa 40:29).

12
UNDER CONSTRUCTION

"But my life is so screwed up at the moment," you say.

Listen, "*Now* are we the sons of God, and it doth not yet appear what we *shall* be..." (1 Jn 3:2).

Ever been to a construction site? It looks like anything but a building doesn't it?

That's because "it doth not yet appear" what it shall be. But bit by bit under the architect's supervision, blocks, beams, wood, and piles of sand start taking shape.

Months pass before there's even a hint that a building is going up – yet it is.

You may be a mess right now.

Indeed when the church is doing its job, there should be lots of "messy people" in it; people being pulled out of tough situations; people in the process of being restored.

Under Construction

No baby comes out of the womb clean and dressed up. Spiritual rebirthing is messy!

But the good news is you *have* been spiritually reborn! You *are* under construction! There *is* a plan and a purpose behind what's going on in your life! Things are coming together. Be encouraged!

You see, when Christ comes into your life, your *spirit* is immediately changed, but your *emotions*, your *appetites*, and your *attitudes* still need work.

In each of us there are areas that need to be made whole. Until they are, we struggle and handle them in dysfunctional and destructive ways.

Those who say, "If you were really a Christian you wouldn't act like that," forget that falling down is just part of learning to walk.

You can *know* what to do, yet struggle to do it.

Sin isn't necessarily the problem, sometimes it's how we "medicate" the problem.

For example, we go out looking for intimacy and end up with sex, or go out looking for peace and come home with a fifth of alcohol. And all the while our real needs are not being addressed.

The answer you're looking for can't be found in

people, things, or substances; it can only be found in a relationship with God.

Real peace comes when you turn to Him in your weakness, and allow Him to do for you what nobody else can. Only *He* can regenerate your spirit. Only *He* can satisfy the longings of your heart.

Only *He* can bring you to the place of maturity and wholeness.

13
ENDURANCE –
THE PRICE TAG FOR ACHIEVEMENT

Success in *any* venture lies in holding on, when others let go. We want instant results; if we don't get them we leave our jobs, our churches, and our families.

This is particularly true of those of us who've spent a lifetime looking for "a quick-fix."

There's a *process* we must go through regardless of our level of faith. There can be no shortcuts. You've got to pay full price – it never goes on sale! If it costs you nothing, it's worth nothing!

Endurance is the price tag for achievement!

Listen, "We pray that you'll have the strength… not the grim strength of gritting your teeth but the… strength God gives…that endures the unendurable and spills over into joy" (Col 1:11 TM).

Did you get that? God will give you the strength to *endure*!

When you're under pressure, He'll empower you to go through it and reward you with joy on the other side.

So hang in there – what God has in store for you is worth any price you have to pay.

14
WHEN YOU'RE TEMPTED TO GO BACK

Most of us are not slow learners, we're just quick forgetters!

Next time you suffer from "Euphoric Recall" and feel tempted to go back to your old habit, tell yourself of these four things.

> (a) *"I won't go back because I don't want to hurt the One I love."* Paul writes, "Christ's love compels us" (2 Cor 5:14 NIV). Instead of saying "no" because you're afraid God will punish *you*, take it to a higher level and say no because you don't want to hurt *Him*. Protect your relationship with God!

> (b) *"I won't go back because the enemy has no right to control me."* Jesus said, "If the Son sets you free, you will be free indeed" (Jn 8:36 NIV). That means being unshackled, unlimited, free to be all that God put you on this earth to be.

(c) *"I won't go back because I deserve better."* Listen: "'For I know the plans I have for you,' declares the Lord, 'plans to prosper you… plans to give you hope and a future'" (Jer 29:11 NIV). Remind yourself daily of God's plans for your life, and don't permit the enemy to threaten or sabotage them by getting you to go back to your old ways.

(d) *"I won't go back because others are watching."* John said, "Whoever loves his brother lives in the light, and there is nothing in him to make him stumble" (1 Jn 2:10 NIV). Others are counting on you – don't let them down. Each victory you win encourages them to believe that *they* can live the overcoming life too!

In his great book, *Spiritual Breakthroughs*, Bruce Wilkinson writes, "I made a dramatic breakthrough when I discovered that *right before* every temptation, my emotions were distressed and that I was actually *seeking for comfort*. That's when I remembered the promise of Jesus, 'I will pray the Father, and he shall give you another Comforter that he may abide with you for ever' (Jn 14:16).

"Incredibly, Jesus gave us The Holy Spirit to be our ever-present source of comfort. I wondered what would happen if I specifically asked Him to comfort me in the time of temptation. I decided to try. I prayed: 'Dear Holy Spirit, I'm in desperate need of you. I don't want to sin – please comfort me now.' At first nothing happened. How discouraged I felt. But then I slowly became aware of something – I felt comforted. I didn't know exactly *when* I was comforted, I only knew that I *was* – that my soul felt soothed and no longer in pain. When I turned back toward the temptation, it had miraculously slid back into the darkness, far away from my senses. I was free!

"I've prayed to my comforter many times since, and discovered two immutable truths: (1) The Holy Spirit always – and I mean *always* – completes His responsibility in my heart. (2) He gives me His comfort within *three minutes*, though I can never put my finger on the moment when He does. I call this prayer for comfort my 'Three-Minute Temptation Buster.'"

Why don't *you* try it!

15
IT'S A DAILY BATTLE

Don't be taken by surprise; the battle begins the moment your feet hit the floor each morning!

Paul writes, "The moment I decide to do good, sin is there to trip me up. I truly delight in God's commands, but…not all of me joins in that delight" (Rom 7:19 TM).

What's happening?

Your *flesh* is at war with your *spirit*, seducing you into relaxing your defenses. The moment you do it'll "nail you." It'll whisper, "Go ahead, its no big deal; everybody does it. Who'll know anyway?"

Learn to identify that voice *before* it becomes a thought entertained, a deed done, a habit reinforced and a life ruined.

Your new birth doesn't do away with your old nature – it just brings it into sharp contrast. You may be redeemed, but you're still living in a carnal body!

It's a Daily Battle

If you try to fight flesh in the power of the flesh, you'll just end up fighting yourself.

What's the answer?

"Walk in the Spirit, and you shall not fulfill the lust of the flesh" (Gal 5:16 NKJV).

How do you do that?

By reading, meditating on, and obeying God's Word – instead of doing what comes naturally!

If you "blow it" occasionally, don't get discouraged!

You've been programmed from birth to walk in the flesh. Now you're learning to walk in The Spirit with a new set of values, new companions, new habits, new priorities, new power, and new management.

Your new birth began a new battle, if you're going to win it you must learn to live in "war-mode!"

Solomon said, "The strong spirit of a man sustains him in…trouble" (Pr 18:14 AMP).

We're each made up of body, soul, and spirit. Our spirit (inner man) is where God comes to dwell. But that doesn't mean we'll automatically have "a strong spirit." No, your spirit is like your body – it must be nourished.

Do you want to develop a strong spirit?

First – spend time each day in God's Word.
Why?

Because it renews your mind and produces Christ-like qualities in you!

Jesus knew the power of Scripture firsthand. He studied it as a boy, hid it in His heart, and through it was able to overcome the tempter in the wilderness. Your Bible will:

(1) Feed you spiritually. Listen, "When your words came, I ate them; they were my joy and my heart's delight" (Jer 15:16 NIV).

(2) Keep you strong in temptation. Listen again, "How can a young man keep his way pure? By living according to your word" (Ps 119:9 NIV).

(3) Make you mentally sharp. David said, "The entrance of Your words gives…understanding" (Ps 119:130 NKJV).

Second – recognise the power of prayer. Listen, "He went up on a mountain side by himself to pray" (Mt 14:23 NIV).

If *Jesus* needed to spend time in prayer – so do you!

John Bunyan said, "You can do more than pray *after* you've prayed, but you can't do more than pray *until* you've prayed." Think about that!

In prayer you commit your life to God, otherwise who's in charge? That thought should bring you to your knees – daily!

Do you want to develop a strong spirit? One that will sustain you in trouble? Then make a commitment each day to spend time in God's Word and in prayer.

Here's a prayer you can pray, especially when you're struggling with temptation and old habits.

Father, I thank You for giving me new life. I am a Christian by faith, help me now to be one in lifestyle. Holy Spirit assist me in becoming all that You desire me to be. Give me the patience I need to go through this process of change. I thank You that while You are changing my habits, Your blood is continually cleansing me. Lord, I promise not to take advantage of Your mercy by continuing in my old ways. It is my earnest desire to change. I confess my sins and shortcomings and repent of them. I surrender my life and my will to You. Grant me Your mercy and grace as I begin today to work with You on the areas that keep me from being pleasing in Your sight. I will not quit. I will not faint. I will serve You as long as I live. In Jesus' Name – Amen.

16
EIGHT "HABIT BREAKERS"

What should you do when you stumble and fall?
Get back up!
Be like the man who said, "I'm never down. I'm either up, or I'm getting up!"
What should you do when the pressure's on and you're tempted to give in, or give up altogether?
Turn to God's Word!
The following eight scriptures are "habit breakers."
Keep them close to you. Use them daily. Commit them to memory. They'll strengthen and protect you in moments of temptation.

(1) "If you think you are standing firm, be careful that you don't fall! No temptation has seized you except what is common to man. And God is faithful; he will not let you be tempted beyond what you can bear. But when you are tempted,

Eight "Habit Breakers"

he will also provide a way out so that you can stand up under it" (1 Cor 10:12-13 NIV).

(2) *"In my anguish I cried to the Lord, and he answered by setting me free. The Lord is with me; I will not be afraid…The Lord is my strength"* (Ps 118:5-6,14 NIV).

(3) *"The Lord will rescue me from every evil attack and will bring me safely to his heavenly kingdom. To him be glory forever and ever. Amen"* (2 Tim 4:18 NIV).

(4) *"I waited patiently for the Lord; he…heard my cry. He lifted me out of the slimy pit, out of the mud and mire; he set my feet on a rock and gave me a firm place to stand…Blessed is the man who makes the Lord his trust"* (Ps 40:1-4 NIV).

(5) *"Because he himself suffered when he was tempted, he is able to help those who are being tempted"* (Heb 2:18 NIV).

(6) *"He has delivered us from such a deadly peril, and he will deliver us. On him we have set*

our hope that he will continue to deliver us" (2 Cor 1:10 NIV).

(7) "Do not fear, for I am with you; do not be dismayed, for I am your God. I will strengthen you and help you; I will uphold you with my righteous right hand" (Isa 41:10 NIV).

(8) "Stand fast therefore in the liberty by which Christ has made us free, and do not be entangled again with a yoke of bondage" (Gal 5:1 NKJV).

New Insights On *Marriage*
From Bob Gass

Are you happy with your marriage?
Would you like it to be better?

The keys are ...
commitment ...
communication ...
compromise.
And you can learn to use them.

If you want to **"spice up"** a dull marriage, **"shore up"** a shaky one, or take yours and **"make it better"** – this book's for you.

A Better Marriage: *Keys to Intimacy and Growth*

Order your copy today. 1-800-964-9846 or 1-678-461-9989

Worry-Free Living

Discover the **"Top Nine"** causes of worry in your life.

Jesus said, "Stop allowing yourselves to be agitated and... fearful." Then He tells us how!

God promises us, "Power to keep ourselves calm in the days of adversity."

Read this book. Access that power. Learn to live "worry free!"

Conquering Worry	**Order your copy today!**
How to Deal with the Stress in Your Life By Bob Gass	Telephone: 1-800-964-9846 or 1-678-461-9989 P.O. Box 767550, Roswell, GA 30076 U.S.A.